For my father, Robert French,
and for Brian and Jennifer Chandler,
Les Hughes (in memory),
and for Mavis Hughes and Jane Hill

Easter
Copyright © 2002 by Frances Lincoln Limited
Text and illustrations copyright © 2002 Fiona French
Printed in Singapore. All rights reserved.
www.harperchildrens.com

Library of Congress Cataloging-in-Publication Data
Bible. N.T. Gospels. English. Authorized. Selections. 2002.
  Easter : with words from the authorized version of the King James Bible / [edited by] Fiona
French.
      p.     cm.
  Summary: Text from the King James Bible and stained-glass illustrations depict the story of the
last week of Jesus' life, his crucifixion, and his rising from the dead.
    ISBN 0-06-623929-X
  1. Jesus Christ—Biography—Passion Week—Juvenile literature.   2. Jesus Christ—
Resurrection—Juvenile literature.   [1. Jesus Christ—Passion.   2. Jesus Christ—Resurrection.
3. Easter.]   I. French, Fiona.   II. Title.
BT430 .A3 2002                                                                                     2001024752
226'.052036—dc21

1  2  3  4  5  6  7  8  9  10  ❖  First HarperCollins Edition, 2002
First published in the United Kingdom by Frances Lincoln Limited, 2002

Fiona French

# Easter

With Words from the King James Bible

HarperCollinsPublishers

When they heard that Jesus was coming to Jerusalem, people took branches of palm trees, and went forth to meet him, and cried, "Hosanna: Blessed is the King of Israel that cometh in the name of the Lord."

Now when the even was come, Jesus sat down with the twelve. And as they did eat, Jesus took bread, and blessed it, and broke it, and gave it to them and said, "Take, eat: this is my body."

And he took the cup and when he had given thanks, he gave it to them: and they all drank of it.

Then cometh Jesus with them unto a place called Gethsemane. And Judas, one of the twelve, came, and with him a great multitude with swords and staves.

Now he that betrayed Jesus gave them a sign, saying, "Whomsoever I shall kiss, that same is he: hold him fast." And he came to him and said, "Hail, master"; and kissed him. Then they laid hands on Jesus, and took him.

And when they had bound him, they led him away and delivered him to Pontius Pilate the governor. And the governor asked him, saying, "Art thou the King of the Jews?" And Jesus said unto him, "Thou sayest."

But the chief priests and elders persuaded the multitude that they should destroy Jesus. When Pilate saw that he could prevail nothing, he took water, and washed his hands, saying, "I am innocent of the blood of this just person: see ye to it."

Then the soldiers of the governor took Jesus into the common hall. And they stripped him, and put on him a scarlet robe. And when they had plaited a crown of thorns, they put it upon his head, and a reed in his right hand: and they bowed the knee before him, and mocked him, saying, "Hail, King of the Jews!"

And as they came out, they found
a man of Cyrene, Simon by name:
him they compelled to bear Jesus' cross. And
they were come unto a place called Golgotha,
that is to say, a place of a skull.

And they crucified him.

When the even was come, there came a rich man of Arimathaea, named Joseph, who also himself was Jesus' disciple: He went to Pilate, and begged the body of Jesus. And when Joseph had taken the body, he wrapped it in a clean linen cloth, And laid it in his own new tomb, and he rolled a great stone to the door of the sepulchre, and departed.

N ow upon the first day of the week, very early in the morning, Mary Magdalene and the other Mary came unto the sepulchre, and found the stone rolled away. They entered in, and found not the body of the Lord Jesus.

And behold, two men stood by them in shining garments, and said unto them, "Why seek ye the living among the dead? He is not here, but is risen."

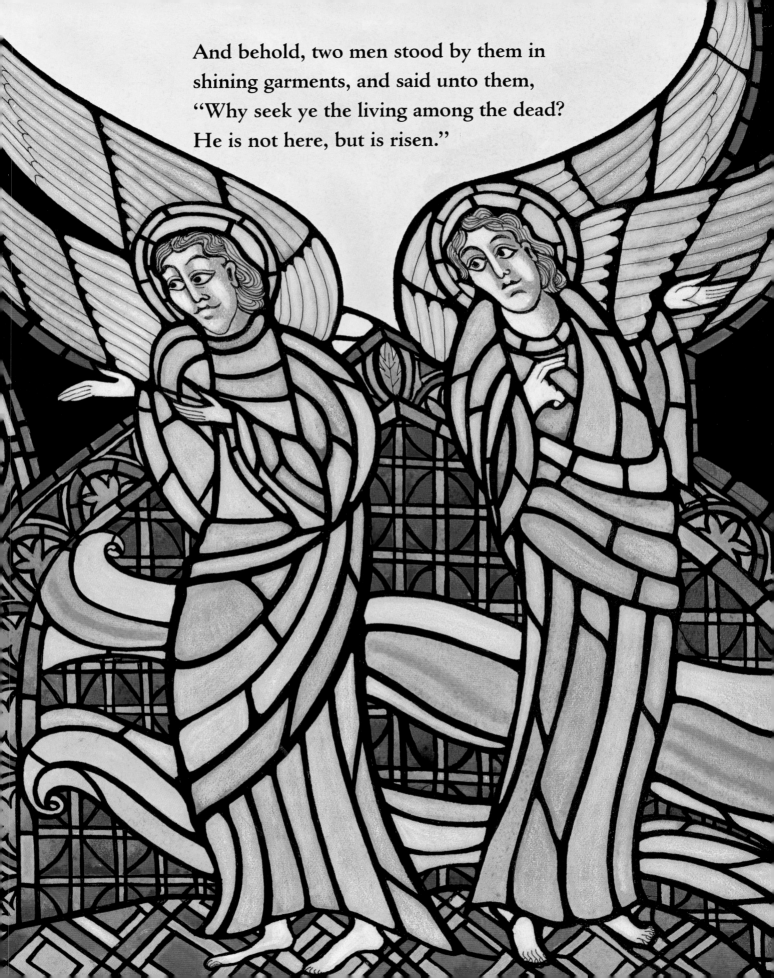

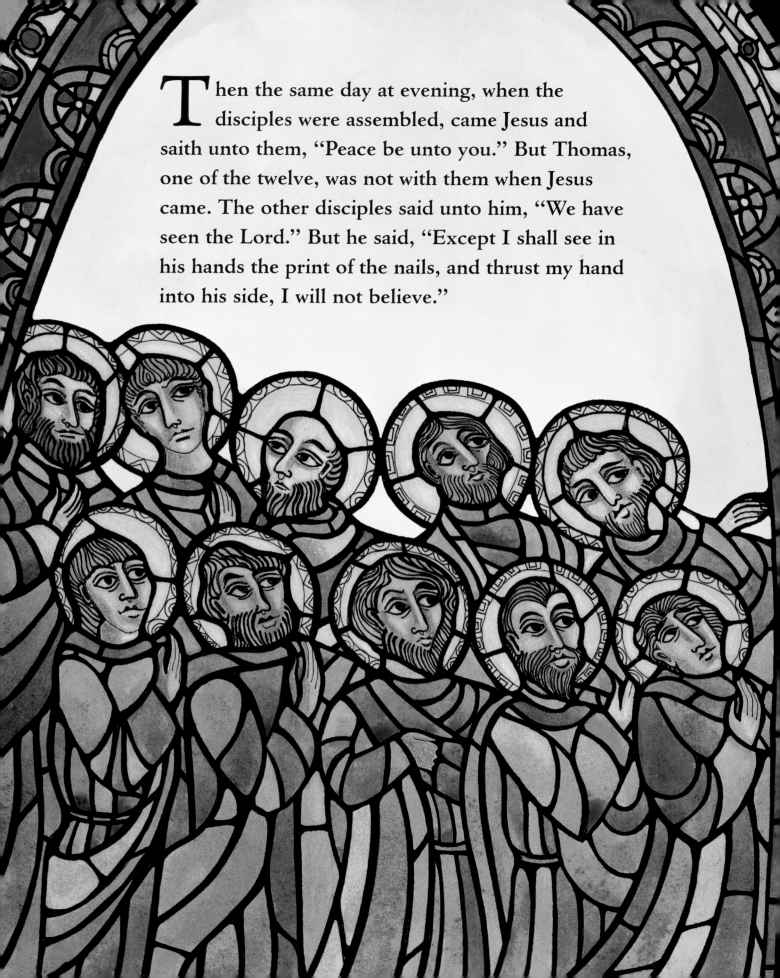

Then the same day at evening, when the disciples were assembled, came Jesus and saith unto them, "Peace be unto you." But Thomas, one of the twelve, was not with them when Jesus came. The other disciples said unto him, "We have seen the Lord." But he said, "Except I shall see in his hands the print of the nails, and thrust my hand into his side, I will not believe."

After eight days his
disciples were within, and Thomas
with them: then came Jesus and stood
in the midst. Then saith he to Thomas,
"Behold my hands, and reach hither thy
hand and thrust it into my side: and be not
faithless, but believing." And Thomas said,
"My Lord and my God!"

Jesus showed himself again to the disciples at the sea of Tiberias. He saith unto them, "Children, have ye any meat?" They answered him, "No." And he said, "Cast the net on the right side of the ship, and ye shall find." They cast therefore, and were not able to draw it for the multitude of fishes.

As soon then as they were come to land, they saw a fire of coals there, and fish laid thereon, and bread. Jesus saith unto them, "Come and dine." And none of the disciples durst ask him, "Who art thou?" knowing that it was the Lord.

And he led them out as far as to Bethany, and he lifted up his hands, and blessed them. And it came to pass, while he blessed them, he was parted from them, and carried up into heaven. And they worshipped him, and returned to Jerusalem with great joy.